More Sight-Word Stories

57 Reproducible Books for Beginning Readers

I will ask my mother
if we can have
something to eat.

by
Gloria Lapin

illustrated by
Becky Radtke

Fearon Teacher Aids
A Division of Frank Schaffer Publications, Inc.

Senior Editor: Kristin Eclov
Copyeditor: Janet Barker
Illustrator: Becky Radtke
Inside Design: Good Neighbor Press, Inc. Grand Junction, CO
Cover Photograph: Nancee McClure

© Fearon Teacher Aids
A Division of Frank Schaffer Publications, Inc.
23740 Hawthorne Boulevard
Torrance, CA 90505-5927

FE7954
ISBN 1-56417-969-9

3 4 5 6 7 8 9

Table of Contents

Introduction

More Sight Word Stories offers an alternative reading program for the beginning reader. The 57 reproducible books carefully and methodically present all 220 Dolch sight words. With the use of predictable text, controlled vocabulary, and frequent word repetition, the emergent reader smoothly glides from the pre-primer level through the Dolch basic sight word list. Additional words have been introduced to enhance the readability of the material. Through the use of rhyme and consonant substitution, the students are also exposed to unlocking words through the use of phonics.

Assembling the Books

These books have been designed with the ease of assembly in mind. Photocopy each book on the front and back of one sheet of paper. Cut each sheet in half along the dotted line. Fold the two sections and slide one section inside the other so that the pages are in numerical order. Staple along the folded edge of the book.

Introduce Each Book

Before beginning, display the cover of the book. Point to the words while reading the title to the child. Encourage oral language by asking the child to guess what the book might be about. Open the book and look at the pictures. Continue the discussion about the book. On each page, ask the child questions that will prompt answers similar to the text. Model the appropriate reading approach by pointing to the words and reading them. Have the child imitate the procedure. It is important for the child to point to the words and say them simultaneously in order to establish the connection between print and sound.

Encourage the child to reread the book several times over the next few days so that the repetition moves the words into long-term memory.

The key to this program is pacing. Give each child time to digest the new words before proceeding. Savor each book, re-read it, discuss the pictures, and ask questions about it.

Master Word List

The master word list (pages 115–116) contains the words introduced in each book. The teacher may choose to present the words ahead of time, or may direct attention to them as they appear in the text, depending on the learning styles of the students.

To a new reader, a capital or lower case letter completely changes the appearance of a word, so both forms are included in the master word list. This provides the teacher with an opportunity to teach different uses of capital letters and to explain how the first letter looks differently, but the word still sounds the same.

Word Cards

Each word included in these books appears on a word card. The word cards are marked with corresponding book numbers where they are introduced. These cards can be cut out and used as is or pasted on index cards for ease of handling.

The word cards can be used after re-reading a book. Encourage the children to locate each word in the story and read it in context. The cards can be placed on a table and the child can identify each, or put them into sentences. They can also be used to play various card games.

Included in the word card collection are sets of words related by phonics. Before beginning phonics instruction allow the child to master the sight vocabulary in the first 12 books. This gives a foundation from which the child should be secure enough to attempt to unlock familiar words. Present only one family of words at a time. Let the child's ability to unlock these words determine the rate of study.

Sentence Strips and Activity Sheets

Sentence strips (pages 125–127) and fill-in-the-blank activity sheets (pages 128–130) have been included to help promote the transfer of learning from one print environment to another. The sentence strips provide additional context in which the student encounters the sight vocabulary. The activity sheets encourage students to choose the more appropriate words to complete the sentences. Use the activity sheets and sentence strips after students have studied the corresponding vocabulary in the books.

Other Activities for Using the Books

- To help children distinguish between units of letters, words, and sentences have them count the words or the sentences on a page.
- Have each child select a sentence from a book and illustrate on another sheet of paper. The child can even change the sentence in some way to extend the story.
- Cut one book into sentence strips and picture cards. Re-assemble the story by matching the sentences and the pictures, placing them in the correct order.
- Copy one of the stories on chart paper. Select words that can be hidden with little slips of paper. Encourage the children to figure out the hidden words using context clues.

Book 8

My rabbit is here.

8

Where Is My Rabbit?

Name ______________________________

1

I see my bear.

6

I cannot find my rabbit.

3

Where is my rabbit?

2

I cannot find my rabbit.

7

I see my dog.

4

I see my cat.

5

A dog can jump down.

8

Book 9

Run and Jump

Name ______________________

1

A girl can jump down.

A boy can run up.

A girl can run up.

2

A boy can jump down.

7

A dog can run up.

4

A cat can run up.

5

The box is big.

8

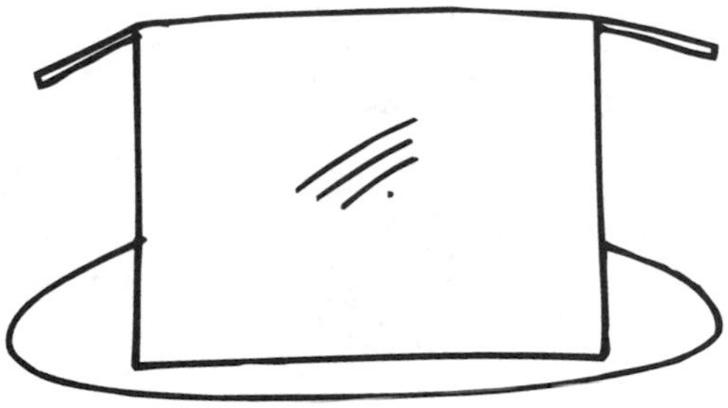

A Box

Name ______________________

1

A rabbit got in the box.

 6

A boy got in the box.

3

A girl got in the box.

2

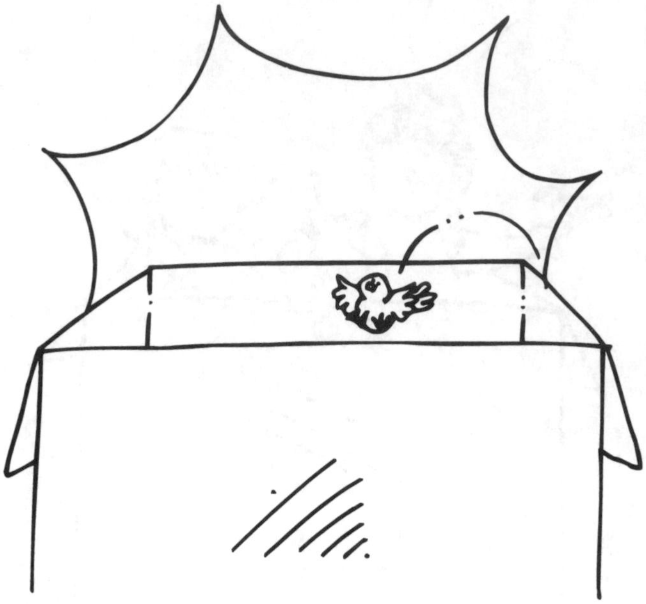

A bird got in the box.

7

A dog got in the box.

4

A cat got in the box.

5

Book 11

You are three
funny dogs.

8

Funny Dogs

Name ______________________

1

I see three funny dogs.

6

Run, funny dog.

3

I see one funny dog.

2

Run, funny dogs.

7

I see two funny dogs.

4

Run, funny dogs.

5

Cats can jump.
Cats can jump down.

8

Book 12

Dogs and Cats

Name ______________________

1

Dogs can jump.

6

Dogs can run up.

3

Dogs can run.

2

Dogs can jump down.

7

Cats can run.

4

Cats can run up.

5

The dog can
see the cat.

8

Book 13

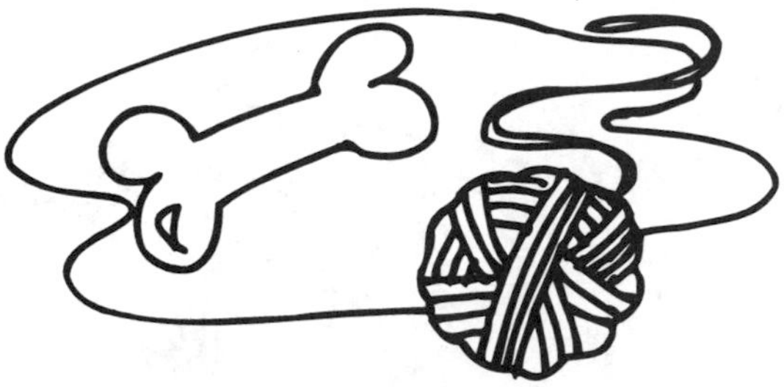

A Dog, A Cat

Name ____________________

1

The cat can run.

6

The dog can run.

3

Where is the dog?
The dog is here.

2

The cat can jump.

7

The dog can jump.

4

Where is the cat?
The cat is here.

5

Book 14

I have a ball.
It can go up.

8

Go Up

Name ______________________________

1

It can go up.

6

It can go up.

3

I have a kite.

2

It can come down.

7

It can come down.

4

I have a plane

5

Book 16

The funny man can
go in my house.

8

We Can

Name ______________________

1

I can go in my house.

6

The dog can
ride a bike.

3

I can ride a bike.

2

The dog can go
in my house.
The cat can go
in my house.

7

The cat can ride a bike.

4

The funny man
can ride a bike.

5

Book 17

Here is the shoe.
Here is a funny dog.

8

One Shoe

Name ______________________

1

The shoe is not here.
Where is the shoe?

6

I cannot find one shoe.
Can you help me
find my shoe?

3

I look funny.
I have one shoe.

2

The shoe is not here.
Where is the shoe?

7

You look funny.
I can help you.

4

The shoe is not here.
Where is the shoe?

5

Book 18

We can run, and
jump, and ride.

8

Run, Jump, and Ride

Name ______________________

1

I like to ride. Do
you like to ride?

6

Yes, I like to run, too.
I can run.

3

I like to run.
Do you like to run?

2

Yes, I like to ride, too.
I can ride.

7

I like to jump.
Do you like to jump?

4

Yes, I like to jump, too.
I can jump.

5

Here I am.
I see you.

8

Book 19

I See You

Name ______________________

1

You go away.
I will find you.

6

Yes, I can ride
a bike, too.

3

I can ride a bike.
Can you ride a bike?

2

Where are you?
I cannot see you.

7

We can ride bikes
to my house.

4

We can play
at my house.

5

The girl is funny, too.

8

A Funny Book

Name ______________________

1

The little dog is funny.

6

Do you want to see my big book?

3

I have a big book.

2

The big man is funny.

7

Yes, I want to see the big book.

4

Come, look. It is funny.

5

You can help me
read the books.

8

Book 21

Books, Books, Books

Name ______________________

1

Books. There are
books in the box.

6

Yes, you can help me.

3

I see you have a big box. Do you want me to help you?

2

There are big books.
There are little books.
There are funny books.

7

Where do you want the box? The box can go here.

4

What is in the box?

5

The rabbit hides. The dog hides. The turtle looks and looks.

Book 22

We Can Play

Name ____________________

"We can hide,
says the turtle.
"Yes," says the dog.
"Yes," says the rabbit.

The dog says,
"I can play."
The turtle says,
"I can play."

The rabbit says,
"I want to play."

2

"You, go hide," says the turtle. "I will look for you."

7

The dog says, "We can ride bikes." The turtle says, "No, I cannot ride a bike."

4

"We can run a race," says the rabbit.
The turtle says, "No, I cannot run a race."

5

The turtle says,
"I want to hide.
Now, I will go in."

8

Book 23

Come Out, Come Out

Name ______________________

1

The turtle says,
"I cannot see you.
Come out. Come out.
I want to see you."

6

The rabbit hides. The
dog hides, too. The
turtle cannot see them.

3

The rabbit, the dog,
and the turtle will play.
The rabbit and the dog
will hide. The turtle will
look for them.

2

The rabbit comes out.
The dog comes out.

7

The turtle looks and
looks. The turtle looks
up. The turtle looks
down. The turtle
cannot see them.

4

The rabbit says,
"I want to get out."
The dog says,
"I want to get down."

5

Book 24

I will get a pet. I like the dog and it likes me. I will get the dog.

Pet Store

Name ______________________________

Look here. I see a mouse. It can go fast.

Look at the pets. I like to see the pets.

I want to go to the
store. I want to see
the pets at the store.

2

Here is a turtle.
It cannot go fast.
It can hide.

7

Come here. Look.
I see a fish. Here
are little fish and
there are big fish.

4

Here are the rabbits.
Can you see them?
They are little.

5

Book 25

What will the frog do? The frog jumps on the dog.

8

Pets

Name ______________________

1

My frog can jump. It jumps to the rabbit.

6

I have a pet, too. My pet is little. My pet can jump, too.

3

I have a dog.
My dog can run.
I have a rabbit. My rabbit can jump.

2

My dog looks at the frog. He wants to see the frog.

7

What is in the box? Is it your pet? I want to see it.

4

You can see it. My pet is not in the box now. My pet can jump out. It is a frog.

5

Book 26

We are here. Here is the store. I will get out now. Can I get a book at the store?

8

A Car Ride

Name ______________________

1

Look! Look! Look what I see. I see a big man in a little car.

6

Yes. I want to go for a ride. I like to go for a ride in the car.

3

I have to go to the store. Will you come for the ride?

2

Look! Look! Look what I see. I see a little girl and a big dog.

7

Get in the car. We will go for a ride in the car. We will go to the store.

4

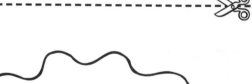

Look! Look! Look what I see. I see a bird in a tree.

5

That was good. I ate it all up. I liked it.

8

Please, Can We Eat Now?

Book 27

Name ____________________

1

When will we eat? Will we eat soon? Will we eat that? Will I like that?

6

We will eat soon.

3

I want to eat. I
want to eat now.
Can we eat now?

2

I like this.
I like to eat this.

7

Please, can we eat,
now? When will we
eat? What will we eat?
Will I like it?

4

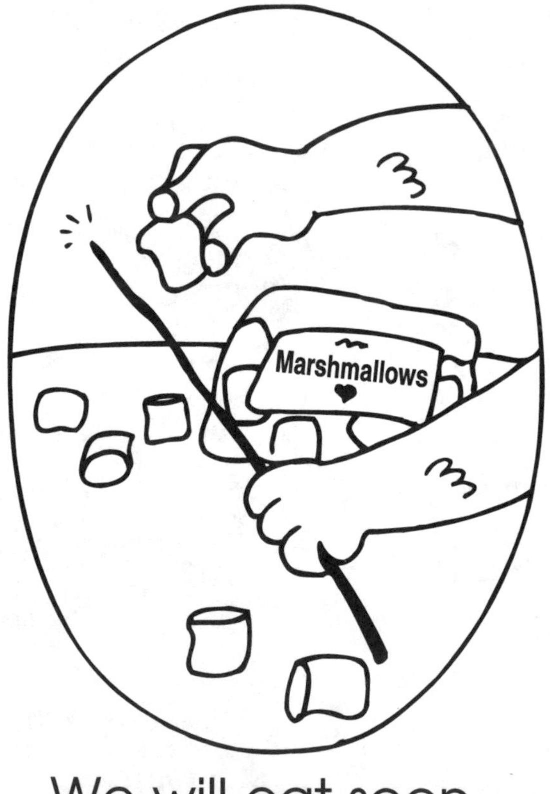

We will eat soon.
Look at this.

5

I liked my dinner.
Thank you. Thank you
for a good dinner.

8

Book 28

I Like My Dinner

Name ____________________

1

Yes! Yes! I will eat
now. This is a good
dinner. I like my dinner.
I will eat it all up.

No one ate your dinner.
It is here. I will get it for
you. Please sit down.

 6

3

Where is my dinner?
Who ate my dinner?
I want my dinner.
I want it now.

2

That was a good dinner.
I ate it all up.

7

When can I eat?
Can I eat soon?
I want to eat soon.

4

Yes, you can eat soon.
Here is your dinner,
now. Please eat your
dinner now.

5

Soon I will eat it all up.
When I go to my house
I will eat it all up.

8

Book 29

What Is Good to Eat?

Name ______________________

1

Look at this. What is it?
It looks good. May I
see it, please?

6

Yes, please. What do
you have that is
good to eat?

3

May I help you?

2

Yes, I like this. I will get it. Thank you.

7

This is new. I like to eat this. It is good to eat. I will eat it when I go to my house.

4

No thank you. I do not like that. I do not want to eat that.

5

Look, here it is. I can wish now. I wish for a new book. I want a new book to read.

8

Book 30

Make a Wish

Name ____________________________

1

I wish for a new bike. My bike is too little. I wish for a big bike. What do you wish for?

6

Yes, I saw it. I saw it go. Where is it now? I cannot see it.

3

Look up there.
Did you see that?
Did you see it go?

2

Where did it go?
It went away. I
cannot wish now.
It went over there.

7

It went over there.
I wish it was here.
I want to see it.

4

Look we can see
it, now. We can
make a wish. What
do you wish for?

5

You say "Please" and "Thank you" like a big girl. You must be a big girl now.

8

Book 31

Please and Thank You

Name ____________________

1

Now you must say "Thank You."

He has a little bear for you, but you must say "Please."

 6

3

Baby, baby come look. Look who came to our house.

2

Thank you for the bear. I like it.

7

Please, may I have the bear?

4

Yes, you may have the bear. The bear is for you so you can play.

5

Book 32

Look at that. It is not
wet now. The sun is out.
It will be a pretty day.

8

A Wet Day

Name ______________________

1

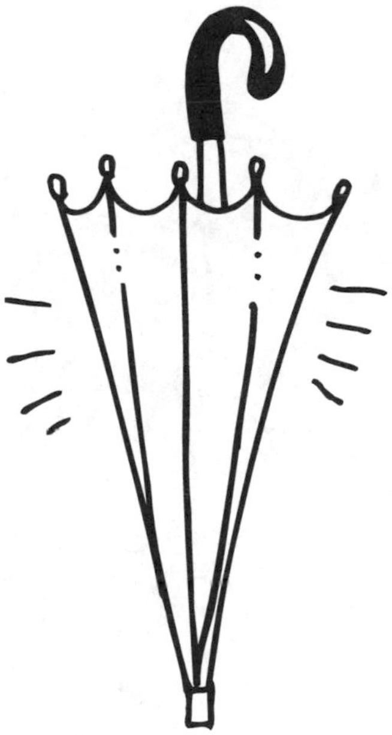

I must take this. I will
walk under this.

6

It will be wet today. I
see it is wet out there.

3

This is a good day. What will I put on today? I will look out and see.

2

It is wet out here. It will be wet all day. I must walk under this.

7

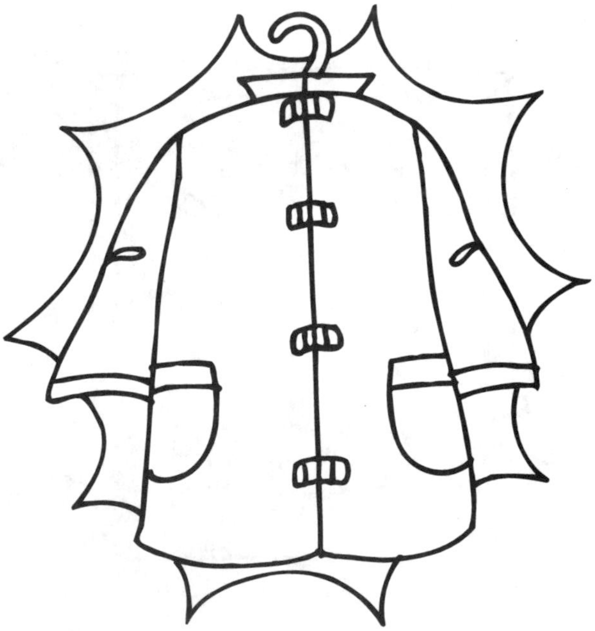

I will put this on. This will help me today.

4

I will put this on. This will help me today.

5

I will be wet, but
I will not be hot.

Book 33

A Hot Day

Name ______________________

I will take this. This is
good for a hot day.

I will look out to see
what I will put on today.

What will it be like today? Will it be a pretty day? Will it be a hot day? Will it be a wet day?

2

I will not be hot here. This is good for a hot day.

7

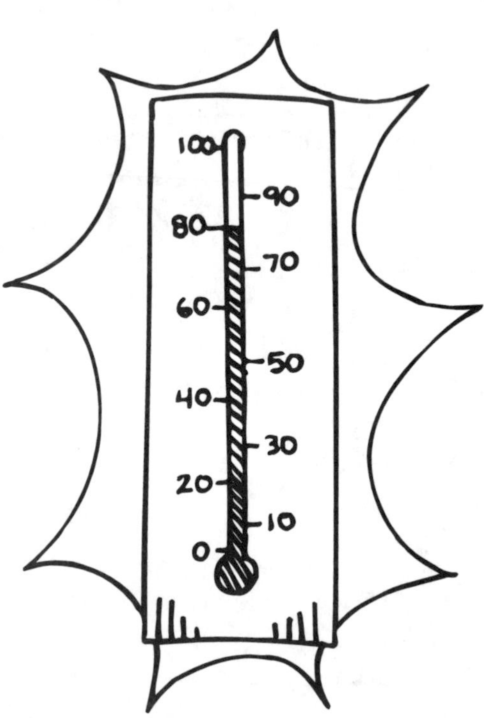

It looks like a pretty hot day. I do not want to be too hot.

4

I will put this on. This will not make me hot.

5

Yes, you can go out,
but come in soon.

8

Book 34

Look Out There

Name ______________________

1

I will put this on. This is good to put on.

My, my. I see what came down. It is all over.

Mother, Mother
come here. Look
out there. Look at
what is out there.

2

I will go out now.
I will run and jump.
I will play.

7

Can I go out? Can
I go out and play?

4

Yes, but what will
you put on.

5

Book 35

Look at the dirt. I see four little plants. The seeds did grow. Now the seeds are plants.

8

Seeds Grow

Name ______________________________

1

Soon the seeds will grow, but not now.

6

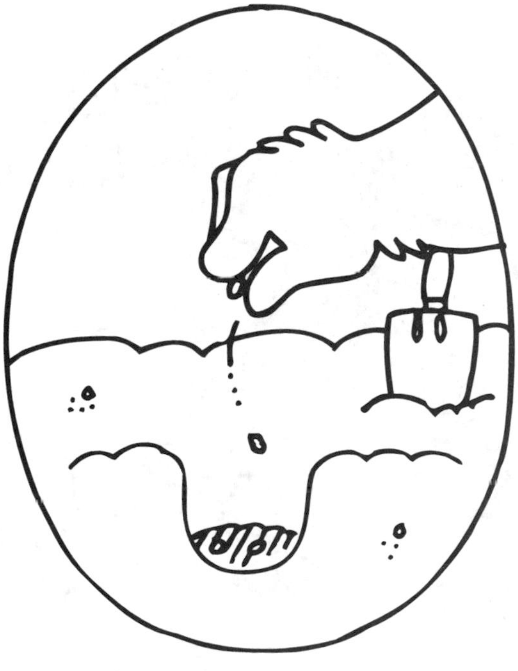

I will put the seeds into the dirt.

3

Here are four seeds. They are little and round.

2

Every day I look at the dirt. Every day I wet the seeds. Did the seeds grow today?

7

I will put the dirt over the seeds.

4

Now, I will wet the dirt and the seeds. I will wet the seeds every day.

5

Book 36

Plants help us live.
Some plants are so
good to eat.

8

Plants

Name ______________________

1

When I give pretty
plants to my mother,
she says, "Thank you."

Plants help us live.
Plants give us food
to eat. I like to eat
food from plants.

I like to grow plants.
Some plants grow big.
Some plants do not grow big.

2

One plant can make this to put on.

7

Plants can help us make a house. We can take a tree and make a house.

4

Plants can make our house pretty.

5

Book 37

Thank you. This is so good. I like our new little pet.

8

A New Pet

Name ______________________

1

Please, may I get this little round one?

6

I see some dogs.
I see some cats.
I see some fish.

3

Every day I go by the pet store. Every day I look in and see pets.

2

Mother, look what I have to give you. It is from me.

7

Today I will get a pet. My mother will like a pet. It can live at our house.

4

I like this little round one. It will grow into a big dog.

5

Book 38

It will grow. It will make new plants.

8

What Is Alive?

Name ________________________

1

It will grow. It makes new birds.

6

A dog is alive. It must have water.

3

What is alive? How do we know when something is alive.

2

A plant is alive. It must have water.

7

It will grow. It makes new dogs.

4

A bird is alive. It must have water.

5

I am alive. It is good to be alive.

Book 39

What Is Not Alive?

Name ______________________

A pot is not alive. It does not need water.

A rock is not alive. It does not need water. It will not grow. It will not make new rocks.

How do we know when something is not alive.

2

It will not grow. It will not make new pots.

7

A can is not alive. It does not need water.

4

It will not grow. It will not make new cans.

5

Now, where am I going to put it? I think I will put it here.

8

Book 40

A Pretty Box

Name ______________________________

1

Yes, I think I will open it now.

6

What do you think is in it? Who is it from?

3

Look! I just got this box.

2

Look how pretty this is. I will have to thank her.

7

I think it is from my mother. It is so pretty, I just want to look at it.

4

Open it and let me see what is in it.

5

Book 41

We went up, up, up.
I like to look down at
all the little houses.

8

Fly Away

Name ______________________

1

I went on an airplane
once. Now I am going
to fly again.

6

Stop that. We are
not going to fly like
birds. We are going
to fly in an airplane.

3

Just think, we are going to fly today. We are going to fly like birds.

2

I think I am going to like it. I am going to fly up there.

7

An airplane is not like a bird. An airplane is not alive.

4

We are going to get into the airplane. We cannot get into a bird.

5

Then one day he got on an airplane. That was the day he could fly.

8

Book 42

I Wish I Could Fly

Name ____________________

1

One day he did this. But he could not fly.

6

Every day he would say, "I wish I could fly."

3

Once upon a time
there was an old man.

2

Every day he would
think of something
new to do. But he
could not fly.

7

Every day he would
think of something
new to do.

4

One day he did this
to a bike. But the
bike could not fly.

5

Can you think of some needs and wants?

Book 43

Needs and Wants

Name ______________________

A TV is a want. We like to look at TV, but we don't need it to live.

A want is something we want to have just because we like it.

What are needs and wants? A need is something we must have to live.

2

A bike is a want. We like to ride bikes, but we don't need bikes to live.

7

Food and water are needs. We could not live if we did not have them.

4

A house is a need because it lets us come in. We can come in from the cold and sleep there.

5

Look at that. The dog found your book. I think the dog wants to read the book.

Book 44

Stop and Think

Name ____________________

Let's go ask if someone saw your book.

Stop and think. Where were you before this? Did you have your book there?

Where is my book?
I don't know where
my book is. I must
have my book.

2

This is where I was
before. I had my
book here.

7

Let me think.
Where was I?

4

I had something to eat.
I had my book there. I
had my book when I
ate my food.

5

We would like
big cookies!

8

Book 45

Something to Eat

Name ______________________

1

The baby is too little
to help. We will put
his toys away for him.
Mother, we put all
the toys away.

I will ask my mother
if we can have
something to eat.

I want something to eat. You look like you would like something to eat, too.

2

Yes, you did. I don't see any toys out here. You can have something to eat, now. What would you like?

7

Mother, may we have something to eat, please?

4

Yes, after you put the toys away, I will give you something to eat.

5

Book 46

I like it best when
he jumps on me.

8

My Dog Sam

Name ______________________

1

If I throw something, he
will run to get it. Then
he will give it to me.

6

He will come
when I call.

3

This is my dog, Sam.
He is the best pet.

2

Sam knows how
to sit up.

7

We both like to take
walks. Sam goes
where I go.

4

We both like to play.
Sam will run around
me as fast as he can.
He goes around
and around.

5

You were right.
You sing very well.

8

Book 47

A Long Car Ride

Name ______________________

1

That is good to sing. It will take a long time to sing it and we have a long time.

6

I like to sing. Do you know how to sing?

3

We are going to ride in the car for a long time. What could we do? We could sing as we ride.

2

You are right. That is good to sing in the car as we ride. Let's both sing.

7

Yes, I know how to sing very well. What would you like to sing?

4

I know what we could sing. We could sing, "This Old Man."

5

It looks like we will not have to walk around. It looks to me like you need to go to sleep now.

8

Book 48

Time for Sleep

Name ____________________

1

Please, let's sing before I go to sleep. I always like to sing before I go to sleep.

6

I don't want to go to sleep. First, I want something to eat.

3

Your mother says it is time to go to sleep.

2

All right. We will sing before you go to sleep. Then we will walk around so you will want to go to sleep.

7

Let's get something to eat. Then will you go to sleep?

4

Please may I have some water first? Very well, you may have some water.

5

Mother gave me five dollars to buy this food. I would like to buy this food. I will take it all to my mother.

8

Book 49

Go to the Store

Name ______________________

1

Mother said to buy apples. How many apples do I need to buy? I will buy five apples.

6

Let me tell you what this says. It says to buy milk, eggs, and apples. Now, walk to the store.

3

Sam, I want you to go to the store and buy some food. I will write down what I need you to buy.

2

Good day, Sam. May I help you today?

7

Mother said to buy milk. So I will buy milk.

4

Mother said to buy eggs. So I will buy eggs.

5

Yes, you are right.
I will wash them
before I eat them.

8

Book 50

The Best Apples

Name ______________________

1

Well then, I think you would like to buy some red apples and some green apples.

6

I will buy some apples Which ones are the best? The red ones or the green ones?

3

I have the best apples.
Come buy some apples.
These are the best
apples around.

2

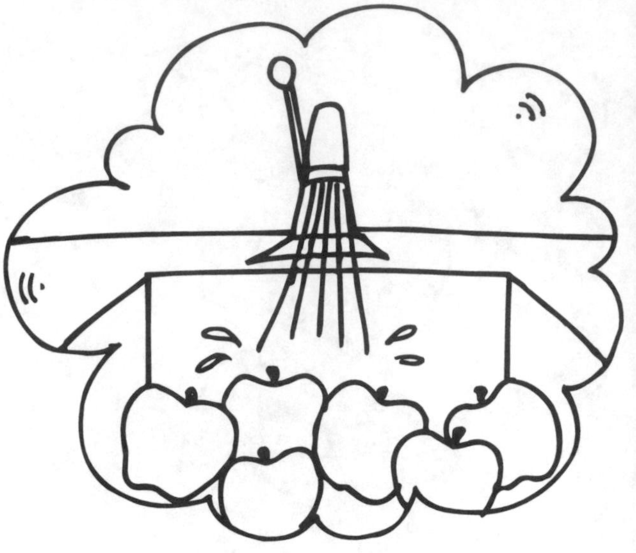

When you get the
apples to your house,
you must wash them.
Always wash apples
before you eat them.

7

Well, which do you
like better? Do you
like to eat red or
green apples?

4

I don't know. I think I
like to eat them both.

5

Well, look at me now. I have mud on my shoes and I am all wet. I think I could get you wet, too.

8

Book 51

All Wet

Name ____________________

1

Here, take this and wash off my shoes.

6

I have been at work. When I was there, I fell in the mud.

3

Where have you been?
Look at those shoes.
Pull off those shoes
before you come into
the house.

2

Stop! I did not tell you
to wash all of me. I said
to wash the shoes. The
shoes are down there.

7

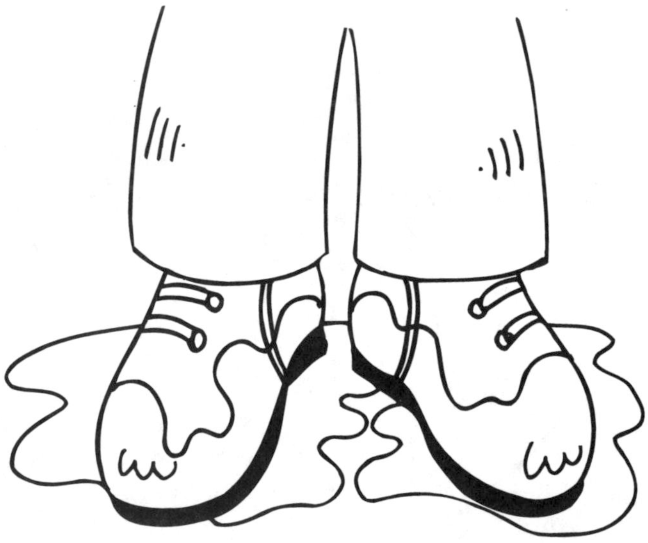

We will have to wash
those shoes when you
pull them off.

4

No, I know what we can
do! I don't have to pull
them off. We can wash
them on me.

5

So the dog helped sing:
"This old man,
He played two
He played 'Knick Knack'
On my shoe . . ."

8

Book 52

Where Is the Shoe?

Name ____________________

1

The dog saw this
old man take the
shoe and play on it.

6

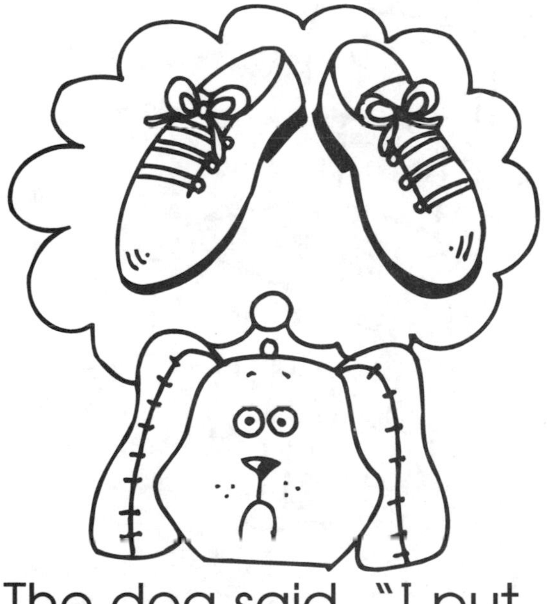

The dog said, "I put
both shoes together
before I went to
sleep. Now I can
find just one."

3

Once upon a time there was a toy dog. It could not find its shoe. It looked everywhere for it.

2

It made the toy dog laugh to see this old man play "Knick Knack" on the shoe.

7

The dog looked here for the shoe. The dog looked there for the shoe. Then it sat down to think about it.

4

The dog looked up and saw this old man pick up the shoe and carry it away.

5

Well, that was good. We had good food and a good walk. Now it is time to clean up. We must do this again soon.

8

Book 53

A Pretty Day

Name ______________________

1

I ate too much. I am so full, now. I must get up and walk or I will fall asleep.

6

It is clean right here. Let's sit down and eat where it is clean.

3

I think today is a pretty day to go out to eat. You pick that up and I will carry the drink.

2

It is better not to eat too much. I only ate a little, but I will walk, too. We can both walk together.

7

I like this kind of food. This is my kind of food. I think I will eat it all.

4

I think I would like some drink. Would you like some drink? May I give you some drink?

5

Thank you. That
is better. You
are a big help.

8

Book 54

A Big Help

Name ______________________

1

Yes, I see where you
got hurt. You got a cut.
First, I will clean it.

6

I went to sit down,
but I fell down. I
think I hurt myself.

3

Why are you down there? It looks like you fell. Did you get hurt?

2

Now, I will put this on the cut. That will keep it clean so it can get better.

7

Show me where you think you got hurt. I will see if I can make it better.

4

I will show you. I hurt myself right here. Hold the light on it, so you can see it better.

5

Book 55

Mother, Mother, look at this. I want to show you what I can draw all by myself.

8

I Can Draw

Name ______________________

1

He would look much better with a small dog. I will draw a small dog with the man. I can draw them together.

6

Yes, I think I will draw. I will start with a small round shape.

3

What shall I do today? Let me think about it. I guess I'll draw.

2

I like this. I think I am done now. I will show it to my mother.

7

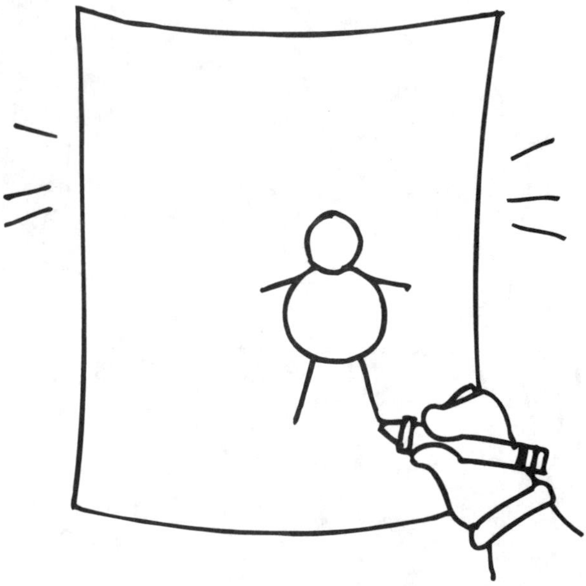

I will draw a big round shape under that. I must draw these, too.

4

I guess it would look better with this.

5

Look at me. Look
at what I have done.
I can ride all by
myself. Thank you
for your help.

8

Book 56

My Very Own Bike

Name ______________________

1

Look how far you went.
You did very well. I
guess you can ride on
your own now.

I will try to ride it by
myself. I don't know
how to ride this kind of
bike, but I will try.

 6

3

Look what I just got today because I am seven. I got my very own bike. I am not six any more. So now I have my very own bike.

2

I don't know if I can. But I am going to try.

7

I can help you ride. If I hold it and you ride, then you will not fall down or get hurt.

4

Thank you. With your help I think I can do it. Keep holding the bike for me. Here I go!

5

You may use my light. Pick something good to eat. Then we can eat and get full and then go to seep.

8

Book 57

A Sleep Out

Name ______________________

1

I would like to eat. I always like to eat. You hold the light so I can get out the food.

6

Will they be warm out there? Did they bring warm things with them?

3

I said the girls could sleep out there. They have to bring their things out with them.

2

Let me use your light because I cannot find my light.

7

I guess they did. If they did not, they can come in and get what they need.

4

This is new for me. I never got to sleep out before. What shall we do first?

5

Master Word List

Book 1
I
see
a
bird
cake
dog
hat
sun
bear
fish

Book 2
big
truck
little
car
dinosaur
cookie
man
baby

Book 3
Are
you
No
am

Book 4
can
jump
You
are
run
We

Book 5
Look
at
me
look

Book 6
Can
said
the
bee
worm
The
boy

Book 7
Where
cannot
in
here
not

Book 8
is
my
rabbit
find
cat
My

Book 9
A
girl
up
down

Book 10
got
box

Book 11
one
funny
Run
two
dogs
three

Book 12
Dogs
Cats

Book 13
—

Book 14
have
kite
It
go
come
plane
ball

Book 15
Sam
where
Come
to
house
Pam

Book 16
bike
ride

Book 17
shoe
help
Here

Book 18
like
Do
Yes
too
and

Book 19
bikes
play
away
will

Book 20
Book
want

Book 21
What
Books
There
books
read

Book 22
says
turtle
race
hide
for
hides
looks

Book 23
them
get
out
Now

Book 24
store
pets
there
rabbits
They
mouse
fast
likes

Book 25
Is
your
pet
it
now
not
frog
jumps
looks
wants
do
on

Book 26
Get
tree
book

Book 27
eat
soon
Please
When
this
that
was
good
ate
all
liked
Will

Book 28
dinner
Who
Thank
That

Book 29
May
Soon

Book 30
Did
saw
went
over
wish
make

Book 31
our
say
may
so
thank
must

Book 32
This
put
day
today
be
take
under
pretty

Book 33
but

Book 34
came

Book 35
four
seeds
round
into
dirt
every
grow
Every

Book 36
Some
live
give
food
from
Plants
One

Book 37
by
Today
new

Book 38
alive
How
know
something
water
makes

Book 39
rock
does
need
pot
pots

Book 40
just
think
Open
let
her
going

Book 41
birds
Stop
fly
an
An
airplane
once
again
houses
Just

Book 42
Once
upon
time
old
would
could
Then

Book 43
needs
wants
because
if
us
cold
sleep
don't

Book 44
were
before
had
ask
someone
found

Book 45
after
toys
his
him
any
cookies

Book 46
best
call
both
walks
goes
around
as
throw
knows

Book 47
long
sing
very
well
Let's
right

Book 48
First
first
always
Very

Book 49
buy
write
tell
milk
eggs
apples
many
five
gave
dollars

Book 50
These
Which
or
better
red
green
wash

Book 51
been
shoes
Pull
pull
off
work
mud

Book 52
its
looked
everywhere
together
about
pick
Knick Knack
laugh
helped

Book 53
drink
clean
kind
much
full
fall
asleep
only

Book 54
Why
hurt
myself
Show
show
Hold
light
cut

Book 55
shall
guess
draw
start
with
small
shape
done

Book 56
seven
own
six
try
Keep
holding
far

Book 57
bring
their
things
warm
never

Word Cards

I	1	dinosaur	2	Look	5
see	1	cookie	2	at	5
a	1	man	2	me	5
bird	1	baby	2	look	5
cake	1	Are	3	Can	6
dog	1	you	3	said	6
hat	1	No	3	the	6
sun	1	am	3	bee	6
bear	1	can	4	worm	6
fish	1	jump	4	The	6
big	2	You	4	boy	6
truck	2	are	4	Where	7
little	2	run	4	cannot	7
car	2	We	4	in	7

Word Cards

here 7	one 11	ball 14
not 7	funny 11	Sam 15
is 8	Run 11	where 15
my 8	two 11	Come 15
rabbit 8	dogs 11	to 15
find 8	three 11	house 15
cat 8	Dogs 12	Pam 15
My 8	Cats 12	bike 16
A 9	have 14	ride 16
girl 9	kite 14	shoe 17
up 9	It 14	help 17
down 9	go 14	Here 17
got 10	come 14	like 18
box 10	plane 14	Do 18

Word Cards

Yes 18	says 22	rabbits 24
too 18	turtle 22	They 24
and 18	race 22	mouse 24
bikes 19	hide 22	fast 24
play 19	for 22	likes 24
away 19	hides 22	Is 25
will 19	looks 22	your 25
Book 20	them 23	pet 25
want 20	get 23	it 25
What 21	out 23	now 25
Books 21	Now 23	not 25
There 21	store 24	frog 25
books 21	pets 24	jumps 25
read 21	there 24	looks 25

wants 25	ate 27	wish 30
do 25	all 27	make 30
on 25	liked 27	our 31
Get 26	Will 27	say 31
tree 26	dinner 28	may 31
book 26	Who 28	so 31
eat 27	Thank 28	thank 31
soon 27	That 28	must 31
Please 27	May 29	This 32
When 27	Soon 29	put 32
this 27	Did 30	day 32
that 27	saw 30	today 32
was 27	went 30	be 32
good 27	over 30	take 32

Word Cards

under 32	give 36	rock 39
pretty 32	food 36	does 39
but 33	from 36	need 39
came 34	Plants 36	pot 39
four 35	One 36	pots 39
seeds 35	by 37	just 40
round 35	Today 37	think 40
into 35	new 37	Open 40
dirt 35	alive 38	let 40
every 35	How 38	her 40
grow 35	know 38	going 40
Every 35	something 38	birds 41
Some 36	water 38	Stop 41
live 36	makes 38	fly 41

Word Cards

an 41	needs 43	after 45
An 41	wants 43	toys 45
airplane 41	because 43	his 45
once 41	if 43	him 45
again 41	us 43	any 45
houses 41	cold 43	cookies 45
Just 41	sleep 43	best 46
Once 42	don't 43	call 46
upon 42	were 44	both 46
time 42	before 44	walks 46
old 42	had 44	goes 46
would 42	ask 44	around 46
could 42	someone 44	as 46
Then 42	found 44	throw 46

Reproducible

Word Cards

knows 46	milk 49	been 51
long 47	eggs 49	shoes 51
sing 47	apples 49	Pull 51
very 47	many 49	pull 51
well 47	five 49	off 51
Let's 47	gave 49	work 51
right 47	dollars 49	mud 51
First 48	These 50	its 52
first 48	Which 50	looked 52
always 48	or 50	everywhere 52
Very 48	better 50	together 52
buy 49	red 50	about 52
write 49	green 50	pick 52
tell 49	wash 50	Knick Knack 52

laugh 52	show 54	six 56
helped 52	Hold 54	try 56
drink 53	light 54	Keep 56
clean 53	cut 54	holding 56
kind 53	shall 55	far 56
much 53	guess 55	bring 57
full 53	draw 55	their 57
fall 53	start 55	things 57
asleep 53	with 55	warm 57
only 53	small 55	never 57
Why 54	shape 55	
hurt 54	done 55	
myself 54	seven 56	
Show 54	own 56	

Sight-Word Sentence Strips

A baby is little.

I am not little.

I see a big man.

My mother is not little.

The dog is in a car.

The dog is out.

The baby is up.

The man is down.

I can run.

You can jump.

Look at me.

I can ride.

The boys run up.

Girls jump up and down.

You can help me read the book.

Do you want to play?

We can run a race.

You can hide and I can find you.

The girl looks for them.

My frog jumps up and down.

I have rabbits for pets.

Did you see Pam come here?

That was a good race.

When will you help me read?

The girl likes to run fast.

May I come over to your house?

I cannot play now.

It is too soon to eat.

Bill and Jill will cook.

Jill took the cook book to Pam.

Bill met Jill on the hill.

I bet you will get wet.

Did the tall man fall in the hall?

Call Pam at the mall.

Pick up the ball and kick it.

The king can sing.

My old ring is gold.

The king sold his old gold ring.

I told you the old man is cold.

How far can the car go?

I need to feed the baby.

If you sell the bell, tell me.

Name ____

1. A girl can jump ______________________. (up, and)

2. My dog is ______________________. (man, big)

3. I can see a ______________________. (dog, little)

4. A boy can see my ______________________. (at, mother)

5. Are you a ______________________? (man, not)

6. I can ______________________. (me, ride)

7. My dog is ______________________. (out, am)

8. I can run and ______________________. (not, jump)

9. Look down, not ______________________. (up, is)

10. Boys and girls can see ______________________. (are, me)

Name ____

1. Boys can ______________________________. (on, read)

2. A car cannot__________________________. (walk, and)

3. I got in the ___________________________. (car, read)

4. I like to read to the _____________________. (am, baby)

5. Boys can walk up and __________________. (said, down)

6. A bird got on____________________________. (me, see)

7. I cannot find my________________________. (rabbit, the)

8. You cannot find ___________________________. (to, me)

9. I am not in the _________________________. (read, box)

10. The boy cannot find the_________________. (baby, and)

Name ______________________________

1. Do you want to ______________________. (go, funny)

2. Where can we ______________________. (little, hide)

3. We can hide ______________________. (there, has)

4. I want to ______________________. (is, play)

5. There is a book I want to ______________. (read, there)

6. Where can I ride my ______________? (bike, out)

7. Can you come to my house to ____________? (play, am)

8. I will help ______________________. (where, you)

9. Can you help me ride my ______________? (sat, bike)

10. Mother reads to the ______________. (here, baby)